Desert Apocrypha

Also by
Zach Hively
———————

Wild Expectations
(with Magdalena Lily McCarson)

Desert Apocrypha

poems

Zach Hively

Casa Urraca Press
ABIQUIU

Copyright (c) 2021 by Zach Hively

All rights reserved.

Thank you for supporting authors and artists by buying an authorized edition of this book and respecting all copyright laws by not reproducing, scanning, or distributing any part of it in any form without permission from the author directly or via the publisher, except as permitted by fair use. You are empowering artists to keep creating, and Casa Urraca Press to keep publishing, books for readers like you who actually look at copyright pages.

Cover art by Zach Hively.
Typed on a 1974 Royal Sabre.

24 23 22 21   3 4 5 6 7

First edition

ISBN 978-1-7351516-7-0

CASA URRACA PRESS

an imprint of Casa Urraca, Ltd.
PO Box 1119
Abiquiu, NM 87510
casaurracaltd.com

for Barrett

and all you teach me, amigo mío

Contents

Five Times Coming Home

I.	Other People	3
II.	In the Arroyo del Perro	4
III.	Untaming	5
IV.	Don't Believe That Time Is a Line	7
V.	This Must Be the Place	9
Apocryphal: Querencia		10

Five Rains

I.	Trinity	15
II.	Virga and the Godlight	16
III.	Under Water	18
IV.	Show Your Work	19
V.	Prayers	23
Apocryphal: Hawkeye Beach		25

Five of the Very Many Analog Pleasures

I.	Petrichor	29
II.	Outrunning Lightning	31
III.	Personal Days	33
IV.	Setting Fire	34
V.	Early Morning, Riverside	37
Apocryphal: I Stepped Off the Trail		38

Five Love Notes to the Universe
  and Everything

I.   To the Secret Life
        of Making New Things   41
II. To the Cryptobiotic Soil   43
III. To the Snake I Ran Over   45
IV. To the Space Flotsam   46
V.   To the Little Black Dog
        at Bode's Gas Pumps   49
Apocryphal: To All That I
              Will Never Know   51

Five Ablutions in Sand
  and Solitude

I.   55
II. Beatitude (of Sorts)   56
III. A Ghost Plant, Blooming
        (for the First Time)
        on the Windowsill   57
IV. coyotes converse in the wash
        outside the bedroom window 59
V.   As Yet Untitled   61
Apocryphal: This Is the Spot
              You Poured Me Tea   63

About the Author   67

"Sweatlodge gave Fox, Coyote's kinsman, the ability to restore life by stepping over any shred of bone or fur left of Coyote. Traditionally, Fox had to step over him five times, the ancient pattern number, but with the arrival of Jesuit missionaries and the acceptance of Catholicism, modern accounts mention only three times, the Judeo-Christian pattern number."

— Jay Miller,
from the introduction to
Mourning Dove's <u>Coyote Stories</u>

Five Times Coming Home

I. Other People

They worry about me being here
as clear as snake tracks in the sand.

As if I will tire
of reading worn stones
and could ever translate
the strata of stories
in the walls sheered off
by guerilla floods
and illuminated by
the roots of cedars,
patient monks.

As if I could ever smell
over the next ridge
to my satisfaction
and finish tallying the stars
on my walls
like the count of my days.

As if I need more
than myself
and the indifferent welcome
of this, my companion land.

II. In the Arroyo del Perro

-- now the sun
strains to grace
the arroyo air
on our midday way
to the dry creek bed.

Does the silt gurgle
and murmur in its sleep?
Does it remember
the flow of water
the way this cottonwood

remembers the straining
sunlight in the undercoat
of its leaves?
Or is this stillness
part of the flow --

-- the little river's
sigh, its exhalation,
fasting on motion
so it can feast
on her return?

III. Untaming

feral mind, feral heart
rocks dirt trees

fire and sky, moon and sun
the flow and ebb

turning toward, drawing away
where is the wild man

the shapeshifter
with smoke and stories

has he forgotten himself here
no mistakes

more serious than joy
reacquainted with feet and hands

find the sky again
grow thick with quiet

continue choosing
turning toward

to feel it all
all ways of being

are not exclusive
lay them bare

again and
always

IV. Don't Believe That Time Is a Line

whatever today's gods and textbooks
might infer.

Time is not
the shortest distance
between
two points.

No no.

It bears us
inevitably, inexplicably
from here to there
through its own
familiar bends
and channels.

It winds us
from there
back to here,
a rhythmically
erratic screw
melting deeper
into cork,

turning me always,
inevitably, inexplicably,
back to you
and to you
and to the you
that not even time
can till
back into the earth
behind me.

V. This Must Be the Place

The raven's wings
whumped the wind,
and I mistook the sound
for my dog's hungry panting.

One ant fell from the cedar tree
into my hammock, and one
became four, and I believed
in spontaneous regeneration.

Out here, the gods wear no masks
except the ones that hide
who they really aren't.
I cry when the Milky Way

spills over my rooftop.
I may have dropped here
like an ant out of a cedar tree,
but even among the vastness,

my size is not
my significance,
my presence
my purpose.

Apocryphal: *Querencia*

My way
is not
the only
way.

I must learn
from other ways
to test and hone
my ways,

to make way
for those other ways
any way
I can.

There is
no right way
to love
this place

or let it
love me back,
to test and hone
me and stun

me with
an evening flower
or a print
in the snow,

to make way
for others
as others
made way

for me.

Five Rains

I. Trinity

ditch water rationed
like wartime milk and sugar
airdropped all at once

mustard in the mouth
bang of a new universe
what delicate blooms

this: the way of things
existing to be consumed
what a violent peace

II. Virga and the Godlight

the rumble and the chumble
    of another rain rolling
never any promises

rain scatters here like buckshot
and a storm a dozen miles thataway

can sweep you away sweep you
under

sweep you far from anywhere which
is only nowhere

if your somewheres are safe and snug
this one though

this one is just north
    on this side of the hills
and the wind pump-fakes
    where it's heading

yet the rain, the rain can't lie
trailing tails of dark kites

and my human mind intimates
I should go inside

but my animal hairs tingle because
this is the time to witness geology

up in the sky
so much faster than geology

earth-side
still all the same principles apply

waves and pressures
shifting the shapes of what was

yet all that pales, as we say,
next to this display of virga

and the godlight
at the end of one day.

III. Under Water

I came home from yours
to a landscape altered.
The way, rerouted.

All this silty mud will harden
like vital organs
leathered in the sun.

Speakers amplify my pulse.
The heart lives underwater.
Thunder in a swimming pool.

Bees are restless in the hives.
This year will be good
    for wildflowers.
Whatever didn't wash away

to the El Rito to the Chama
to the Rio Grande to drown
in what's left of the Butte

or end up entombed
under leather
has a hell of a start.

IV. Show Your Work

Let's see:
a generous guess of eleven inches

a year, on approximately fourteen
hundred square feet of metal

roofing, and dismissing what drips
loose where the sun has warped

the gutters -- that gives us
one thousand two hundred eighty-three

cubic feet. We are American; let's
convert that to gallons. More than

I thought: one cubic foot is seven-
   point-four-
eight gallons, for nine thousand

five hundred ninety-six point
   something something
total on the roof. On average.

Let's round down for evaporation
   and forget
about the inevitably exacerbating
   effects

of a changing climate, and call it
nine thousand gallons a year.

Let's see:
I can picture a gallon of milk, or

a five-gallon bucket. But not nine
thousand. So here goes. It would

take this roof nearly seventy-
four years to fill an Olympic pool.

If water burned like gasoline, the
roof would provide a lifetime supply

for a new Subaru, but my
little blue pickup would have

chewed through the gas before
    I even bought
the thing. Let's humanize it: if I

were an average person (according to
the USGS, a fine arbiter of normality),

I would use this year's roof water
indoors alone

in just three months.
We're used to going three months

without significant rain, period. So
in this hypothetical, it's a good thing

I have a well dug. Bonus:
    that water comes
with complimentary arsenic and lead

and uranium, and gratitude that
    at least
it doesn't have jet fuel pluming

toward the pump from a decades-
long leak.

Let's see:
given all this data, plus
    the extraneous

fact that reverse-osmosis water costs
    forty cents
a gallon at the nearest convenience

store or twenty-five an hour's
    drive from here

(in either a Subaru or an old
    true-blue pickup), deduce

the value of waking in the night
    to the orchestral
warm-up of raindrops pinging on that

metal roof –– the value of that scent
    far more eloquent
than the dry and clinical "whiff

of ozone" –– the value of the shimmer
in the low spots that this time

is not a mirage –– the value
    of an afternoon
lullaby of boom and shush.

V. Prayers

Talk is cheap
and the rain barrels run dry
down to the spigots.
Sand holds very little here,
grudges or memories
or last month's monsoons.
We cannot be pure, organic atheists
when we dare the clouds
to back up their bluster.

Prove your might greater
than lightning! and thunder!
and winds muscling through
the window crack
to draw down the blankets!
What have you done for us lately,
lording those storms
     plump to bursting
like fresh-packed wineskins
over our heads?

Let them flow, if you're so wise.
    Drink!
and let the excess drip off your chins
as gluttonous creeks run high
from the mountains.
Do more than spit
on our upturned cheeks
— do more than dirty our cars,
you cowards,
you bastards.

Who are you to decide
who drinks
and who withers!
You could give freely
what the earth charges dearly.
The rain barrels run dry
down below the spigots,
and we do not all boast taproots
that run so deep.

Apocryphal:
>   *Hawkeye Beach*

my own private name
silly because he prefers the water
silly because why would I think
that some soft stretch
should outlast my dog

should outlast any of us
in a land where the sand
models itself after water
which itself kisses our foreheads
before tearing us up by the roots

once every ten years,
or every twenty,
long enough to lull me into learning
the patterns in this place
well enough to give them names

and imagine spreading ashes
so I throw the ball into the water
instead of on the beach
because he prefers the water
that will bury us all

Five of the Very Many Analog Pleasures

I. Petrichor

A teacher of poetry
told my class
that "crustacean"
was not a word
for poetry.

So now I must wonder
what other words
do not belong in poems.
Umbilical, perhaps.
Tartar. Refrigerator. Electrolyte.

But then I learned
about the word
for that smell
of new rain
on a dry sidewalk.

It smells the same
here, with no concrete,
only dust and sun-
strained winds —
and I stopped wondering.

That smell mashes
the four elements
fire air water earth
into a dusty elixir.
Of course it has a word.

Of course
it falls short
of poetry.
The teacher was right
with the wrong word.

Petrichor does not
belong in poems
because
it is pure shorthand
for a spiritual breath

and is therefore
beyond poetry
for people like us
who accept its
wordless ecstasy.

II. Outrunning Lightning

Deep night, I switchbacked the car
into the Black Range in the Gila Forest.
Headlights brushed the dynamited cliffs
and sturdy guardrails —
and a mountain lion.

She tensed and leapt
to the rock face's forehead
before I froze.
She turned to stare —
and I died, but for glass and steel.

I remember my place
whenever I measure up
the thick clouds, stick a finger
in the wind, and consider —
if I can outrun lightning.

My predatory ancestors
were also hunted. They all
survived long enough
to beget me —
wind blew at their backs.

My mind seeks a cave.
My heart says wait one moment more.
Let's make this
a fair race, it says --
let's see what we're really made of.

III. Personal Ways

Listen:

Pry apart the barbed-wire fence
and keep on going up and in
until the walls climb straight
and you run out of slot canyon.
Turn around
and come out again.
This time through,
you'll find a young elk's antler.
Pick it up.
It is not petrified, yet,
but it's closer to stone
than you are.
How does it feel to fall away
land in the sand
replace yourself
but keep your shape
--- no purpose but to take up space
for millions of years?
Ah, fill yourself
with the spit and grit of the earth
and transform some minerals
into something more than stone.

IV. Setting Fire

I don't want
the world
to burn.
I just want,
sometimes,

to light the ship
that holds
my life
and push
it out

to sea.
I can't let go
of everything
I've made,
but I sure could

strike one
little spark
and let
it do
the letting

go.
I could
watch it
turn all
my trials

and triumphs
into heat
and charcoal
and nothing more
nothing else

nothing less
nothing left
but a
residual glow
and a few

vague memories
of the fireworks
show.
Wouldn't that
feel good,

sometimes?
Instead,
I trim
the dead
cedar branches

and feed them
to the clay
chiminea
in the
mornings

when I want
to slow down,
when I want
to smell
a little

like fire
to warn
my world
that I
know how

to set it.

V. Early Morning, Riverside

The first cottonwood leaves
turn in the warm chill. This
is when I like to come
to the river best:

the whole world, yellowed.
I want a cup of coffee
and I will wait for it.
I want to frame this air

on my wall and then
walk through that frame
and live there forever, where
my dog can swim

to the other bank and the grass
licks my toes til the sand sticks.
I want to remember
like I do right now

that it doesn't matter where
we sleep -- gravity tugs
us to the ground
just the same.

Apocryphal:
I Stepped Off the Trail

to find a tree
— any tree would do
— so long as it hid me
from puritan eyes
— and I found
not hiding there

the kind of rock
with green bedded between
white-stippled black
that says
thank you for listening
that hums

you are where you need to be
that whispers
tuck yourself in your pocket
alongside me
and take yourself
wherever you go

Five Love Notes to the Universe and Everything

I. To the Secret Life
of Making New Things

(with thanks to V. B. Price)

The physical world of atoms
    and molecules
plays by a separate rulebook
than the world of our mindscapes.
Alchemy is a metaphor
of understatement. Who bothers

turning lead into gold
when you can turn graphite
into stories, mythologies, entire
lives lived over and over again?
Or wood into spoons,

sand into glass,
mud into houses?
Plenty of people. That's who.
Every being has the creative kernel
at the core, but the life

of making new things remains
so secret precisely because of what
it does not demand we make.
Sense. Money. A difference.
What freaks practice dark magic

in the woods for no wicked purpose
at all? Making newts out of
reeds and twigs for the pure love
of newts doesn't fit in the world
as it is.

It's no crime to fill your belly
off your gifts and your hard work.
All of us who live our own
secret lives understand how
the worlds bleed together.

But even the fellow secretkeepers
cannot know the secrets of another's
magic. It is at once precious,
as individual as personality,
and easy —

never flippant, costing nothing,
the only free lunch in the universe:
creating anything at all
from nothing at all
and creating our selves the same way.

II. To the Cryptobiotic Soil

My friend warned me
"Keep off the kryptonite!"
How could I correct her?

Correctness is blunt and tiresome
any time that calls for more spirit
than precision --
    and the only precision

you require is in my footsteps.
Once I learned to recognize
your black crust not unlike

hail-pelted peat, I also learned
you build yourself slower
than Rome and stand longer

than Tenochtitlan, billions
of microbial denizens linked
like a barrel of monkeys

holding the earth together,
elegant spires as tall
as my knuckle, defying

wind and hoof and recovering
the ruts spun by assholes on ATVs.
I leap from hassock

to hassock, the old hot lava game.
If I fall into you, my foot
won't melt, but I will lose

a sliver of myself
the same way I do
when a bird smacks

the window. I might trade
all the flowers in all
the meadows

just for one
vast untrodden plain
to call your own.

III. To the Snake
     I Ran Over

I did not mean to.
My lane was ending,
I wanted to get in front,
and I wandered

to your side of the stripe.
You were sunning.
So brazen, to warm your blood
so near the white line.

I was too late to swerve
and never even felt you.
Looking back, you might've
already been smushed.

You might even've been
a stump of rope.
I did not stop to check.
What could I do?

I am sorry I am so human
and so unlikely to understand
daring that white line
from the other side.

IV. To the Space Flotsam

Let us take as given
that the elements
have been here
since the beginning
-- yes, uranium downgrades

to lead and so forth
and such like, but the pieces
are all here,
ever since they weren't.
The times

out of all the times
that I feel most elemental myself
are the nights I sit with the dog
under the preferred
    overhanging cedar
on the cooling ground

and we watch the stars.
Is this what gurus and guides
mean by Oneness? I am one element
stacked on another
stacked on another

all of them together
    wearing a trench coat
to pass as human.
But these thoughts are grandiose,
and I am just selfish.
I like how this feels

so I do it.
And when I see a star shooting,
my wasted moments
become elements of the dance.
Here I am, here we are

and who cares if the star
is no meteor at all
but just some piece of space debris,
satellite flotsam
burning up

upon re-entry?
Its elements are like mine,
stacked on another
stacked on another
and choosing to flash and flare

at the very moment
I choose to wait for it
before going to bed.
Shall we?
I ask the dog

and we climb
the back steps
to the house.

v. To the Little Black Dog at Bode's Gas Pumps

This is the stop known for states
around — <u>the</u> stop — the only
stop — full stop — I gas up only
when heading north but I'll come
fill up on water and burritos —
though really I come to see you —
see you mark tires of cars from
all the contiguous forty-eight —
yes even mine — even though
you've collected New Mexico a
thousand thousand times — see you
materialize at the post office
across 84 — never seen you cross
the asphalt — suspect you
wormhole it — used to think you
were lost — dropped out of your
wormhole from somewhere else —
needed to get home — may be we
all think that the first time or
four — but no begging for scraps
— no melty eyes baiting for
affection — you are home — and
I come for you to advise me —

contentment pooled like sunlight
-- like wind nuzzled in sails --
in ears bigger than you are -- as
big as your coolness -- you might
have no name but you have every
thing I could want -- that I
could want and truly need.

Apocryphal:
To All That I Will Never Know

It's not fair —
that I should have to give
one second
to paying bills instead
of asking you questions.

Do crows drink water, or
(like gorillas)
do they hydrate entirely
off their food? How about
that one crow

with the gap-toothed wing?
How can she fly so straight
with a busted piano key
where a feather should be?
Does she drink the creek

or lizards' blood?
And what does she think
of me, shouting
good morning to her
even in the afternoon?

It's not fair —
that I should have to die
one second
before I can even think up
every question I might have.

I like to hope that
when I die, my questions
will perch
around me like
all the books I never read,

like all the crows
with all their opinions
and questions of their own,
and they will flank me
to the underworld, or

to the afterlife, or to the next
life, or back to the source
of nothingness — to
one question, if things were fair,
that I'd like to answer for myself.

Five Ablutions in Sand and Solitude

I.

This desert gets inside you
like a lover's secret voice --

hair tufted on a miniature bone
left in a discarded road --

rocks worn smooth as mantras
by water that is never there --

the dog barks at threats
    I will never understand
because he keeps them at bay --

then he lays himself on the couch.

These, I think,
must be clues to the mystery.

What good are prayers without
birds out the window, anyway?

II. Beatitude (of Sorts)

The arroyo tells stories here
with more breath than verbs.
Her languorous code
lulls me into
suspecting she's sleeping.

Meanwhile
I can listen to the bunny tracks
and the tire tracks,
the flow of ghost water
sorting sand into threads,
snow clinging to the shadows
under heedless grass.

Silence is not static,
and she whispers my own tracks
back to me,
dry echoes of your feet
consecrating other earth with mine.

III. A Ghost Plant, Blooming (for the First Time) on the Windowsill

Leave no trace
— what a soothing lullaby.
We can walk this earth only
if we leave our footprints.
We have no other way.

Songs of dinosaurs
still ripple in the rocks.
We have not forgotten nature.
We simply forget
that we are nature,
always will be,
no matter how many
shoes we wear
to shield
our senses.

What to do with such primal knowledge?
What to do but remember?
Some may collect dry bones
and carve prayers in skulls again.
Deify certain among the stars
and return the old gods
to their terrestrial feet.

Eating my daily bread
with pine sap loitering on my palms
— that revives the mystery,
for me, at least,
and these ascending flowers
reflect my own
neglected secrets.

IV. coyotes converse
    in the wash outside
    the bedroom window

chirps and chirrups and
    full diatribes
eloquent and veiled to me

but i can feel them

feel their thoughts
their caws and croaks

as if i could subtitle them
    with charcoal

as much a part of me as
    monkey babble
perhaps even more so

for i don't belong here
not eerie howls echoing
    and filling hills
as with oatmeal stained thick
    by blueberries

but ritualistic rhetoric
gods conversing with the earth
    that built them

i need to start collecting rocks
    again
bringing the dirt to this side
    of the window
until sides don't matter at all

just like they always haven't

and my own cackles and coos
turn tufted ears up and down
    the wash
and the conversation gets one
    person wilder
and the gods remember my name too

v. As Yet Untitled

The raven on the juniper
barks me
back to my work.

I'm not here
to earn an existence
or dream of someday dreaming
dragons' dreams atop
a midden pile of
precious waste.

The earth lumbers
— lumbers deep, deep,
turning always to seasons
and oblivious to trifles
and changes.

If the blue whale,
the largest a creature can be,
aspired any grander, its heart
might burst from
being so much.

Who am I to think
I might ever be
more than myself,
recklessly whole?

Now the raven on the juniper
puffs its insistent throat.
Takes off between the trees.
Now, as always,
is the time.

Apocryphal:
This Is the Spot You Poured Me Tea

The table you set,
while I did dishes.
The butcher-block counter
you pressed me up against
well after check-out time,
the shower we took together
as a given.

Perhaps I shouldn't revisit
the scenes of my joys.
Rituals don't have to be
the result of long habits
worn into stone, polishing
wood, wearing tracks.

Once
is all it takes.
Once,
to cast the old and hard
parts of living
into wild and tender
sacrilege.

The canonical pieces in Five Ablutions in Sand and Solitude first appeared in the Sacred show at the Magdalena Lily McCarson gallery in Santa Fe in February 2020.

"Other People," "Don't Believe That Time Is a Line," and "This Must Be the Place" first appeared in <u>Trickster</u> (2020).

"This Is the Spot You Poured Me Tea" first appeared in <u>Banshee</u> 11 (2021).

"I Stepped Off the Trail" first appeared in <u>Conceptions Southwest</u> 44 (2021).

About the Author

Zach Hively writes poetry and creative nonfiction. His Fool's Gold column has twice earned first place from the Society of Professional Journalists' Top of the Rockies awards, and he has won a Maxwell Medallion from the Dog Writers' Association of America. He writes music and performs with Oxygen on Embers and is the author of <u>Wild Expectations</u>, with photography by Magdalena Lily McCarson. He lives near Abiquiu, New Mexico.

You can read selections and learn more at zachhively.com.

Casa Urraca Press

We are a home for words that speak to the soul and stimulate thought. We publish daring, eloquent authors of poetry and creative nonfiction. And we offer workshops with our authors and other artists.

Every writer and every publisher has a slant. Ours tilts toward the richness of the high desert, where all are welcome who manage to find their way.

Proudly centered somewhere near Abiquiu, New Mexico.

Visit us at casaurracaltd.com for exquisite editions of our books and for workshop registration.

www.ingramcontent.com/pod-product-compliance
Lightning Source LLC
Chambersburg PA
CBHW020302030426
42336CB00010B/869